Burlesque and Bequest

Rewriting the Inheritance of Women

Cat Cuevas

Savannah Broadway and Jerome Virnich, editors

ISBN-10: 1500874949
ISBN-13: 978-1500874940

Printed by CreateSpace
Available from Amazon.com, Createspace.com, and other retail outlets.

CONTENTS

Acknowledgments   v

Introduction   1

Afrose   9

Barbara   17

Eveta   21

Kate   31

Katie   37

Katy   43

Kelly   51

Nicole   57

Kate   63

Cat   69

Your Story   73

DEDICATION

To all women, and the spirit of the feminine in everyone.

"A story is not just a story. In its most innate and proper sense, it is someone's life. It is the numen of their life and their first-hand familiarity with the stories they carry that makes the story 'medicine.'"

— Clarissa Pinkola Estés, Ph.D., *Women Who Run With the Wolves*

"What eclipses people's greatness? What stops us short from being as creative, caring, and resilient as we are? What is it that squeezes the life out of us so stealthily that we volunteer to shrink to a shadow of our true selves? And most importantly, how do we stop it?"

- Victoria Castle, *The Trance of Scarcity*

ACKNOWLEDGMENTS

My deepest gratitude to everyone who has shared their stories with me. Special thanks to Afrose, Barbara, Caitlin, Iris, Jennifer, Kate, Kate, Katie, Kelly, Leslie, Mary J, Nicole, Nora, Eveta, Holly, Sierra, my Sinner Saint Sisters, Gnosis, Play it Forward, my family, my friends, and my lover. May our stories transform one another, and the world.

INTRODUCTION

The Cat

I'm Cat Cuevas. My legacy is to lead the restoration of humanity. My mission is to welcome, cultivate, and exemplify the potential in human relationships. I'm a leadership consultant who coaches organizations through critical transformations, and a co-owner of the Sinner Saint Burlesque dance company.

I am a ferocious self-critic. I struggle escaping a paradigm of scarcity and being 'good enough.' I despise being out of control, and I don't say 'I love you' as often as I should. My biggest regret is that I bullied my siblings when I was young. No matter how many times I tell myself that all women have cellulite, I still hate it. I don't go a day without experiencing street harassment. Seafood makes me gag. Embracing my imperfections is an ongoing challenge.

I am a feminist, activist, teacher, and healer. I am a recovering Army brat, a ballroom dancer, and a big sister. My favorite way to lose myself and find myself is through dance. I love second glasses of wine, helping people discover their joy, traveling the world, and learning to become a better human being. I want to exemplify feminine leadership. I am a catalyst for transformational change, and love being marvelous.

My 'work' and my '*Work*'

I have always been fascinated with how people get along. I aspired to find a profession where I could help create high-performing teams and healthy relationships. In high school and college, I was obsessed with sport psychology, John Wooden's pyramid of success, and Vince Lombardi quotes. There was, however, one distinct moment when I became crystal clear about the work I wanted to do. It was the moment I realized that THIS IS MY WORK. Not the job I wanted to have. Not the next stepping stone to success. My soul had been called to action, and my profession became my purpose.

It was the last semester in undergrad, and I was cruising through my final Contemporary World Affairs class of the year. We watched a documentary, called *Long Night's Journey Into Day*, which included stories of apartheid in South Africa. It was the Amy Elizabeth Biehl story that really knocked me off my feet. Amy was an American graduate student and anti-apartheid activist in her mid 20's. She was brutally murdered in August 1993, just outside Cape Town. Listening to her story, I felt overwhelmed with rage and sadness. But what happened next stirred my soul awake.

Four people were convicted of killing Amy. In 1998, they were pardoned by South Africa's Truth and Reconciliation Commission. Amy's parents, Linda and Peter, petitioned in favor of their pardon. After the hearing, Amy's father shook the murderers' hands, and reportedly said, "The most important vehicle of reconciliation is open and honest dialogue ... We are here to reconcile a human life which was taken without an opportunity for dialogue. When we are finished with this process we must move forward with linked arms."

Amy's parents started the Amy Biehl Foundation Trust to empower youth and prevent further violence. Two of the men convicted of Amy's murder joined her parents, and went on to work for the foundation's programs.

I was confounded. Never in my life had I heard of such a radical act of compassion and reconciliation. I didn't even know humans were capable of that magnitude of empathy, forgiveness, and healing. That is the power of stories.

At that moment, I KNEW. I knew I had to experience this capacity for compassion and transformation. I knew I needed to teach anyone and everyone how to do it too. I knew it could change the world. In a brief moment, I understood the complexity and the potential of human relationships.

I went on to earn my MA in International Peace and Conflict Resolution, where I was flooded with information about the causes and impacts of violent conflict. Afterward, I established a niche in education. I taught community leaders, educators and children around the world social skills to prevent violence and to resolve conflicts peacefully. I returned to graduate school years later, and earned another MA in Leadership and Organizational Development, where I learned more systemic ways to build healthy organizations.

As a consultant, I focus on leadership psychology. I teach businesses and community organizations about the human dynamics that impact peak performance, create workplace joy, and help serve the global good. I encourage economics for peace, and teach leaders the skills needed to liberate the power of human relationships.

From C-Suite to Striptease

In addition to being a leadership consultant, I am also a co-owner of Sinner Saint Productions, a burlesque dance company. Sinner Saint's mission is to celebrate the human experience through smart, sexy entertainment. Burlesque is a wildly popular, outrageously sexy, and deliciously fun style of performance art. It uses humor, politics, music, and striptease to tell stories and entertain audiences. Sinner Saint tours internationally, performing narrative cabarets, creating neoburlesque theatre, and teaching workshops.

Our troupe's philosophy is that burlesque, and striptease, empowers women to employ their bodies to tell their personal stories. We use burlesque to challenge internalized and institutionalized oppression, to contest the social-political landscape, to evoke joy, and to embrace our feminine sexuality. Though we engage audiences through entertaining and humorous performances, our passion is in helping women heal the wounds of patriarchy and misogyny. We help celebrate all that women are capable of by exemplifying prototypes of female liberation.

Many burlesque performers have a unique character they play on stage—an alter ego. My alter ego, is Doña Dei Cuori. The word "Doña" is an Iberian and Italian title of royalty, while "Cuori" means heart. Doña is Cat on glamorous steroids – the most exuberant, confident, wild, and regal version of myself. Through Doña, I can become any person I choose. I've portrayed Amelia Earhart, Catherine the Great, Rosa Parks, and the Furies. I've discovered gravity, freed myself from body shame, faced my shadow self, and summoned wild beasts. Doña gives me permission to embody and reveal any facet of myself. She allows me to unapologetically stretch beyond the confines of my day to day life.

It is not often you hear the words C-Suite and striptease in the same sentence. Often I've wondered: as a woman, can I be a sexual being AND be taken seriously at the top levels of organizations? Damn right I can! My performance pieces explore the power and primacy of female leaders. I create characters that are playfully political, flirtatiously foxy, and cunningly cosmopolitan. I've learned more about business leadership from being an exotic dancer than from any of the business journals I've ever read.

The Show - *Inheritance: Maiden, Mother and Crone*

In the fall of 2014, Sinner Saint produced a full-length theatrical show, called *Inheritance: Maiden, Mother, Crone*. The show is an ensemble neoburlesque performance, but it's not a play. It's brazenly political, but it's not a protest. It's the unification of performance art, intergenerational dialogue, feminism, Beloved Community, and contemporary archetypes. It's also one of the main inspirations for this book.

The *Inheritance* show was intended to ignite some of the most important conversations and questions of the century:

- How can we celebrate, exalt and integrate the feminine?
- How do we help this generation of women insist on themselves and their self-worth?
- How do we collectively declare a new legacy for women?
- How do women build relationships with men that promote liberation and healing for us all?

Inheritance: Maiden, Mother, Crone was designed as a living will and testament. It details what we hope to bequeath to other women, and the world. The show challenges some of the most basic and pervasive assumptions about womanhood, power, and the structure of humanity. It imagines what life would be like if the wholeness, health, and experiences of women were universally celebrated. My troupe sisters and I craved a glimpse of this world, so we decided to give collective birth to it. We refused to wait for someone else to show us how to do it. We demanded it from ourselves.

With the socio-political backdrop colored by debates over reproductive rights, rape culture, the wage gap, street harassment, and educational opportunities, *Inheritance* became more than a show. It became a sexual, social, and spiritual revolution for us and our audiences.

The Stories that Matter

Inheritance: Maiden, Mother, Crone aims to share a world where the feminine is integrated and celebrated. I wrote this book to inspire further conversations about what it means to be a woman. My hope is that by listening to each other's tales, women can change the fabric of our collective stories and re-author a better world. Our stories will become our inheritance, our history, our mythology, and our legacy.

Stories are sacred. They are the seeds of internalized oppression, desire, joy, worthiness, shame, and sacrifice. This book is a collection of stories from women who pioneered the folklore of their souls. May this book serve as a guide for you to awaken your own legacy.

On the surface, this book will explore the real-life tales of what it means to be a woman: what we learn, what we teach, what makes us laugh, what makes us cry, what makes us furious, and what we hope for.

As you listen deeper, however, you will begin to hear that which rings true in all of us. You might recognize the shadows and shame we hide. You may be familiar with how women prevent themselves from living into greatness, how we learn to love those restraints, and how we inflict them on one another. Chances are you know how hard it is to question your own existence, self-acceptance, and self-worth each day. You may also recall the bliss and triumph of living authentically. These stories belong to all of us.

Why I'm Creating this Book

I am creating this book to help myself (and others) rewrite the lies that have become ingrained in our narratives. In speaking with women, and listening to their stories, I started to notice some of the falsehoods that I tell myself. Here are some examples:

- I am responsible for everyone else. My happiness, needs, wants, and dreams are secondary.
- My intuition isn't valid.

- I am not powerful.
- I must be strong all the time. Vulnerability is weakness.
- I am not good enough.
- I am too much.
- My sexuality is my highest value.
- I am not complete without a partner. I need to be in relationship to feel validated.
- I should not love and accept myself. I am not worthy of love.
- My self-worth is determined by others.

When did THAT become my life's story?! Once I recognized I could change these stories, I became free to declare the truths I want to see. I want a world where:

- A culture of dehumanization is not tolerated.
- Feminine leadership is looked up to in business and politics.
- Women have agency over their bodies.
- Everyone can grow up without body shame.
- We can heal from internalized oppression.
- I can walk down the street without being sexually harassed.
- We know we are good enough, and we are worthy of love.
- Women insist on their economic, social, spiritual, sexual and political power.

I am writing this book to share the stories of courageous women who are taking a stand against the stories they've inherited, and declaring new truths. They are changing the legacy of what it means to be women. I hope this book inspires you to reveal your story, to listen to the stories of others, and choose the stories you want to live by. Every story matters. Once women join together like this, it will evoke a revolution.

A Book, a Show, and a Revolution

The *Inheritance* movement is where my work with feminism, performance art, leadership development, and social justice converge. As breakthroughs often do, the inspiration for this project hit at a time when I was stressed, desperate, and out of work.

It had been a year since leaving my last job, and I decided to ask the Universe what I should do for work. The Universe replied in an abrupt and mildly impatient tone. "You've been looking for the wrong thing," it said. "You shouldn't be looking for a job or new clients."

I stopped breathing for a moment. First, I just heard a big booming voice. Woah. Secondly, in some tucked away corner of my soul I knew the voice was right. Maybe I wasn't finding a new job because I wasn't supposed to be looking for one. A painfully real and terrifying moment of clarity swept over me. Predictably, I inquired, "Then what I am supposed to…"

The voice replied sharply, "A leadership uprising. A new form of revolution. The evolution of revolution."

At that moment, I had the opportunity to question both my survival (how am I going to make money?!) and my sanity (now I'm hearing big booming voices?!). Step one, nix the job search. Step two, sign me up for a revolution. Step three, seek spiritual counseling.

My spiritual counselor and I turned to the all-knowing Google oracle. We searched for the etymological foundations of the words evolution and revolution. The roots of 'evolution,' we discovered, were grounded in 'opening out,' 'unfolding,' and the 'development of something from a simple to a complex form.' 'Revolution', coming from the root revolver, referred to 'rolling back,' and to cycle around an axis.

My purpose suddenly became clear. I was to initiate the rise of an opening out and unfolding of a rolling back and return to cycling. What the hell?! The only things rolling back were my eyes in my head. In my confusion, I did the only thing that made sense…I posted this message on Facebook. What did I get back? Thirty-five 'likes,' a handful of folks signing up for this revolution, and a colleague reminding me that, "When you ask the universe, you are really asking yourself." The Facebook is wise.

It all made sense, somehow. The show, this book, and the ripples of conversations thereafter are a new type of revolution – one that will evolve from the inside-out. The revolution is a show. A process. A dance.

7

A story. A book. A movement of invincible vulnerability. A sisterhood. An opening out of the heart. An unfolding of the soul. A revision of the truths we live by. It's a new inheritance. It's the declaration of a new legacy for women.

The stories shared in this book are reflections of identity, vulnerability, authenticity, and the humanity in all of us. Together, I hope we can compassionately close chapters that no longer serve us, and approach one another's stories with curiosity. Once we do, we can begin to understand how our stories were forged, update them, and pass on an inheritance that will better serve us, our elders, and our children.

What follows is a collection of those stories, and a guide to exploring your own. To the brave women who shared their stories, I want to express my deepest gratitude. I am so profoundly inspired by how you strive to live your lives authentically, and insist on your own greatness. Hearing your stories, your struggles, and your triumphs help us all to remember the importance of our own.

I see Afrose as a vivacious, wild, and spiritual woman. She is connected to the source of her own curiosity. Afrose is both expansive and deeply reflective: a writer, poet, traveler, and free spirit. I admire the way she allows her feet to carry her, though she may not know where they lead. She embodies a soft yet unapologetic trust in herself that I envy. Afrose prompts me to honor the wisdom of my authentic self. She reminds me to trust my creative power and let my intuitive, self-healing body guide the way. Legacy is meant to be lived, not left.

AFROSE

Fort Worth, Texas, 1984
Tornado, barefoot, unruly, raven, frog, Queen of Pentacles, confused, reaching, buzzing, illuminating, restless, afraid, courageous, wild, alone, apart, searching, dark, impulsive, creatrix.

What I've Inherited

I inherited from my parents the tradition of not settling down, staying in one city for two years at most in my adult life. I used to not like this, would fight against it, but I've come to terms with being rootless, without a home. Fighting against my gypsy nature made me miserable because I ended up a housewife, totally inauthentic to my true self. I'm making up for lost time, for the limitations I put on myself because of an ex-husband who hated travel, and I'm spending the summer in France and Brazil. My soul grows through travel, a psychic recently told me, and I think she is right. It's been incredibly healing so far, and I know the journey is far from over.

I've inherited the passion of fiery women who buck against restrictions. They aren't always successful—sometimes the odds are stacked against us. But I told my sister before she passed away that I thought the previous generations of women in our family were trying to push us up to the place she and I had finally reached, which is a financial and material independence. We inherited the task of achieving emotional independence, and I am proudly setting myself to this task.

I love the ornate, gaudy, and ridiculously decadent jewelry I have inherited from my mother, most of which I will never wear in my life and will sit quietly in a bank safe deposit box. But I keep a string of pearls, very treasured in Hyderabad where my family comes from, and I wear

11

them with gothic t-shirts with the sleeves ripped off, ladylike dresses and business casual blazers alike.

An Inheritance I'd Like to Return

I've inherited weak knees and hips. I went to a healer recently, an osteopath, who ultimately concluded that there is nothing physically wrong with my body. It is rather the effect of emotions stuck in the joints that I have not allowed myself to feel. I think everyone in my family does this: does not allow themselves to feel their emotions, express them, release them, and the result is that the emotions make us sick, kill us. My sister died of nonsmoker's lung cancer at the age of 35. One could argue that she had been the most health conscious of all of us, and yet I am told that in Chinese medicine they say grief lives in the lungs. I think she had a lot of grief that she hadn't been able to let go of. I'm working on living in my body, not dissociating and dealing with emotions with integrity for the first time in my life.

The great irony is that I've also inherited a tobacco addiction from my father. I started smoking at age 15, just like him. It's not just an addictive personality that I have been handed, but also a self-destructive streak, a strong saboteur within the subconscious. I love my body, want it to be strong and a tool of my art, but I seem to get in my own way at every turn.

What It Means to Be a Woman

It means having a ridiculously strong creative power in my belly. I was raised Muslim and yet I have always had a very strong connection with the iconography of the Virgin Mary, which I have only allowed myself to explore recently. I had a dream before I set out for France that I had somehow achieved immaculate conception and was in a refugee camp in occupied territory. It was very reminiscent of the time that I spent in occupied Palestine. When I came to France, I found myself randomly in a tiny village with a church that houses one of the few statues of a pregnant Virgin Mary. I took it as a sign, that I needed to explore the creative power that is mine. It is a power that has been feared by men and women alike for centuries. I am afraid of it, too, but I think it signifies a healthy respect, and I'm trying to not let that get in my way.

Being a woman today is such a difficult task. I've been thinking about how many women of my age and milieu are not getting married, not having children, and getting divorced quickly if they do get married. We live in a post-second wave feminism world where women are supposed to be content with prioritizing careers, not needing long term partners, etc. And yet that flies in the face of hundreds of thousands of years of evolution: the biological imperative to find a mate and reproduce. I had an abortion ten years ago. It broke my heart, and I've never come to terms with my biological capacity to create life. I've always wanted children and now have resigned myself to the possibility that I may never have my own. And yet I am in a place in my life where I know I need to attend to myself and not a family for the next several years if I am to reach my potential.

I was a tomboy when I was very, very little until it was shaken out of me. I remember having to manufacture crushes on boys at school in order to fit in. I accepted that little girls were supposed to want to be Disney princesses. By the time I had made myself into something more feminine, I was introduced to feminism. And then a whole 'nother set of conflicting messages came into play: don't be weak, be smart, be independent, be fierce and sassy.

A lot of this has played out in terms of my own gender expression. I have oscillated wildly between very feminine self-representation and extremely androgynous over the years. I've finally settled with a blend of the two that has been working for me quite well for the last few years, but I have a feeling that this external negotiation symbolizes just the beginning of me reckoning with my own femininity.

What I Want to Get Out of Being a Woman

I guess I can't imagine not being a woman, so this question feels difficult to answer. The question really says to me, what do you want to get out of life? I want to reach my highest self in this lifetime. I know that's a tall order. What does that look like? I want to dance, to sing, to write, to heal, laugh, cry, and live really, really deeply.

I want deep connection. I noticed when I wrote the list of words that described me, none of them really describe me in relation to others. And I feel displaced, disconnected. Without community. But I am at the point where I realize I need to work on myself a little bit longer before I can invite that deep connection into my life. I was speaking to a friend the other day, someone I consider a soul sibling. He told me about how an elder had told him that he was a son of their community, even though he sometimes struggles, and brings that onto the stage of their church. It made me cry immediately, because I realized that I don't have that and I desperately want it.

Part of this connection is the sense of really being seen. I've felt invisible my whole life. I've carefully developed an outer persona of being larger than life, the center of attention, competent and generous, funny and cordial, and that persona is real and true and part of me. But only a part. Because I know there is more there, the Shadow that I think no one could possibly love. Except perhaps me. I'm hoping my own love will be enough.

Something I Regret

I don't allow myself to have regrets. If I have them, I don't feel them. I did use to wallow in them until age 19—I regretted not doing better in school, having wasted time re-reading the same silly fiction when I could have been diving into subjects that would make me a more interesting person, etc. But at 19 I found myself in an emotional abusive relationship, and, after a lot of struggle, I got myself out of it. Alone. Other people were critical of this boy in my life, critical of how I isolated myself from my friends and family, but no one saw what was really happening, and no one helped me out. After it was over, I realized that even though I was mad at my friends and family for not helping me, I needed to get out on my own, in order to learn the lesson I needed to learn. To command more respect for myself. To know that I am strong enough to survive even my closest partners turning on me. Now I always look at everything that happens as a blessing, as the fire that forges the steel in my spine and gives me strength. I've been able to thank the universe for its abundance. Even for the loss of my sister. It wouldn't have been such a loss if she hadn't had been such a blessing in my life, such a radiant force in the lives of hundreds of people. Her death was a call to live each day fully, to be my authentic self, even though that self really scares me. And I've answered that call.

The Legacy I Want to Live

I believe as a writer that I don't really create anything myself. I am not the Source, but I can be an open channel to the Source. I can lower a bucket into the well and just see what gets dragged up. I can get it down, rather than think it up, as Julia Cameron says in the Artist's Way. I need to get out of my own way and let this process unfold. I don't know exactly what that legacy looks like concretely, but it's there in the written word. It's written on the inside of my eyelids, on the other side of the sky, to paraphrase Neruda.

Barbara was my advisor and mentor in graduate school when I studied international peace and conflict resolution. She introduced me to transformative mediation, peace education, and what I now call emotional intelligence. This forever changed my life and my relationships. Barbara is a pioneer in the peace and conflict resolution field. This foremother fought many uphill battles, so I can empathize with her believing that because she is a woman she needs to prove herself. I often wonder who I am trying to prove myself to. Why do I need someone else's permission to think I am good enough? The real answer: I need their endorsement because I have not yet approved of myself. I believe their judgment of my worthiness supersedes my own. Yikes—a difficult realization to swallow. This is a piece of inheritance I want to return.

Barbara and I share the desire to leave the legacy that peace is possible. I believe that before we can bring peace to the world and value the lives of each other, we must first learn to value ourselves. I must learn to value myself.

BARBARA

Philadelphia, Pennsylvania, 1952
Following my calling to be a peacebuilder, I am teacher, a leader, and a feminist. I hold a vision for equality that is my driving force.

What I've Inherited

I have inherited my work ethic from my mother. She lived most of her adult life with multiple sclerosis, worked full time, and raised four children. She never let anything stop her. She did it all with a sense of humor and a need to gain power over her disease.

An Inheritance I'd Like to Return

My work ethic! I work even if I am in pain. I recently fell on the ice and broke my hip and my wrist and had to spend two weeks in the hospital. I had such a drive to work from my bed to make sure I was not missing any deadlines. I should have spent more time resting than worrying.

What It Means to be a Woman

What being a woman means to me is to be proving I can do the job no matter what. I have to work harder and be smarter than my male counterparts in the non-profit community. It means always being on guard so that you don't slip up. It means being the emotional glue for my family. It means carrying guilt when your kids are upset. It means feeling pressured to try to make everyone happy. I recognize that I need to take time for my spiritual growth and feel very supported by my community of women friends to do this. I feel as if I need to be the mediator, or the healer.

What I Want to Get Out of Being a Woman

At this point in my life: becoming an elder. I want to mentor other women of all ages so that I can continue to learn and grow as I contribute to their learning and growth. It is mutually beneficial! I seek happiness and playfulness, wisdom and spiritual growth.

Something I Regret

I try to live my live with no regrets, as that causes suffering. Instead, I look at all the mistakes I have made as important failures that have helped me to become the person I am now.

The Legacy I Want to Live

The legacy I want to pass on is that peace is possible. I want to model BEING PEACE. I love passing onto my students the knowledge I have gained in my almost 30 years of peacemaking.

Eveta is one of the courageous souls I met in my first burlesque class. I am in awe of her self-awareness and grace. When I talk to Eveta, I feel cradled and comforted by her wisdom. After interviewing her, I spent weeks wondering how I can help women embrace their greatness. Not another day can go by that women refuse themselves and their worthiness. Whatever it takes, women must start insisting on themselves, trusting themselves, and believing in themselves. If one generation of women could do this…my god…the earth would move. THIS is the revolution. Practice repeating it with me: "Not another day will go by that I refuse my worthiness. I trust myself. I believe in myself. I insist on myself." Say it until it feels good, and until it sinks into your bones.

EVETA

North York, Ontario, Canada, 1970
Brave, curious, beautiful, intelligent, ambitious, ambivert, independent, creative, adaptable, stressed, wounded, genuine, guileless, strong, considerate, self-critical, passionate, lost, optimistic, introspective.

What I've Inherited

Luxurious hair and resilience. Well, my hair has given me a few opportunities to shine (no pun intended) and it contributes to my feeling beautiful, and, to a degree, shielded. The idea of shearing it all off comes up from time to time, and has happened once before in my adult lifetime. I wanted the longest hair as a child, but was not allowed to grow it so. My father preferred above the shoulder cuts on my sister and I, and my mother obliged by giving us hybrid bob/bowl cuts.

Now I'm on the cusp of doing it again, but maybe not. The radical shearing of most of my thick, long hair off does make me feel quite vulnerable—honestly it's a kind of 'naked' feeling. But it's still so tempting at this point in my life (divorce, relocation, professional limbo)—like shedding an old skin, a cleansing, a deeper ritual of renewal and rebirth. There's a new layer to this now too, something I have referred to as "embracing the crone." You see, I have quite a lot of silver coming in. I'm fascinated and enamored with it and yet not certain I am ready to embrace it just yet. I'm a young 43 after all. I hear my mother telling me it's not proper for women of a certain age to have long hair. I've always been puzzled and frankly annoyed by this, and often have challenged her as to why she would think that, let alone preach it. Her mother, whom I only met a few times, had very long grey hair that she often wore in a single braid down her back. I liked this about Grandma,

23

this and the fact she remarried in her 80s with the giddiness of a head-over-heels school girl. So anyhow, if I cut my hair short now I will also be silver. It's simultaneously scary and exciting. That's hair—I love my hair. My sister got the lightning speed metabolism and 20/20 vision; I got the uber thick hair and cute nose. I do sometimes think, "Oh my god, I am going to start dating soon, in my 40s. Should I dye my hair?"

Resilience, on the other hand, I had to initially dig to identify. My mother has a lot of fear, and we are very different people. She also has a lot of shame about where she comes from (poor, under-educated, immigrant family). I struggled to think of something more of my character that comes from her and her side that I carry with me. As a result, I started to ask a few more questions about her side of the family. I found out that she had started some genealogical research a few years ago, but abandoned it when her brothers had been angered with some claims and stories that were uncovered. She happily handed the file over to me and as I spent some time wide-eyed and pouring through the bits and pieces — names, dates, old letters, passports, records, a photo or two etc. I realized that my grandmother, great grandmother, my mother and her sisters, they all had really challenging lives.

Immigration is no easy transition! I know this just emigrating from Canada to the USA, let alone traversing the ocean and making home in a new country with a different language and little in the way of a thriving economy. Working the land and being a rural farmer's wife is hard-work. Birthing and raising 10+ children as my great-grandmother and grandmother did is unimaginable (and some did not survive as infants). It must have been terribly isolating, sacrificing, punishing more times than not. I started to come to a deeper appreciation of the drive and resilience behind their survival; their fortitude. I recall my mother's tale of when their farmhouse burned down; she and her 12 brothers and sisters and parents stayed in the barn while the house was rebuilt by them and the community. OMG 'raised in a barn!' Sayings certainly can cut deep.

Of course Mom and I are very different; we've had very different lives! But despite hardship my mother has a heart of gold. Her love is endless and her generous, tender nurturing extends to most anyone in need—except herself. What resilience—to keep moving forward in life, to seek connection, to love family, stay healthy and active. The women of my family fall, get knocked down, and then get right back up. What a gift of legacy to have as an undercurrent. If it can be brought out into the light I would like to think that it might mitigate the shame of what was not had, achieved, etc. etc. This resilience seems to be the tether that bridges the maternal generations of individuals in my family.

An Inheritance I'd Like to Return

Shame and self-denial. I received a lot of messages of shame as I grew up and a lot of it was bodily based. My parents had both been virgins when they married in their early 20s; sex was taboo and shameful, as was nakedness or anything suggestive of the same. My father was absent from all conversations that would touch on this, except telling me that if I "did it" before I was 16 I'd be dead (the assumption being by his hand). My mother was painfully uncomfortable and unfamiliar with her own sense of self and her sexuality—her discomfort around the subject was tangible. I recall a time when I was around 12 years old and walking around the house in my father's old collared shirt, like a dress. My mother admonished me sternly and told me it was inappropriate to be dressed like this even in our house. What I wore was the subject of much fighting as I grew up—the message being that I must remain 'proper'. I thought most of this was bullshit. So I'd pack my tight jeans out of the house to change; I'd use indelible marker to make my hair blue or red, etc. And I got in trouble often. It wears you down over time. The unspoken message sinks in.

I was opinionated and outspoken as a child and was met with a lot of resistance. Yet in trying to know myself, make choices, and feel worthy I was either denied, over-ruled, or left to my own to figure these things out. My father was very controlling and my mother was happy with this arrangement, whereas I was not. I was often told what my name would have been had I been a boy, a son. Instead I was named after my paternal great-grandmother who I never met. None of this served to instill a sense of who I was but rather the token I was; symbolic of something or someone else—another's memory, my parents' unfulfilled dreams and desires.

I wanted a mentor but my parents wanted a compliant, well-rounded daughter. Well-rounded meant music lessons, dance lessons, sporting activities, and straight As academically. I was adventurous enough to try it all, except when asked what instrument I wanted to learn and I responded with "drums" I got accordion, piano, organ lessons. When asked which sport I wanted to do I said "horseback riding" and I was signed up for a softball team, a bowling league, and one season of curling even. I did like the bowling and eventually persisted my way to horseback riding camp for a summer. I have a bronze medallion in tap, took jazz and baton for years, and very briefly ballet—all because I had to, and hated every parade I had to don a leotard and go and march and twirl through the streets. My first high school report card had 7 A's and a D in typing ... I was simply told I could do better.

On the upside I really learned what I don't like, but on the downside I think I also learned to devalue what I really wanted because somehow it just didn't matter. What all this seems to mean to me today comes from a reflection on the fact that I am always challenging myself, always reaching for the next accomplishment. And yet I'm not certain how to gauge what I really want, where fulfillment lies. It's like I'm too out of practice to trust the impulses or know what that is, or worse, I don't believe I quite yet deserve what I really truly want so I keep trying to prove myself in the meantime.

Through the process of my recent divorce, my mother was very weepy and told me she just wanted me to be happy. I want her to know that while this process is painful, these steps are me reclaiming my happiness. I don't want to wear her fear. I am renegotiating being seen for who I am. It is a challenging and worthwhile process, to make amends with her and appreciate who she is versus who I want her to be—and vice versa. As much as she hurts for me based on her fears, I hurt for her compromises. I hope we can land together, where we both actually are rather than where we hope the other to be.

Something I've realized through my divorce is how disconnected I'd become from my body. Embodied experience is so key. We walk around unplugged from what we need or feel. The more connected we are with what we need and nurture, the closer we can get to what we want. It is hard to remember how to want for yourself. There are many internalized voices that aren't our own, and we filter through them before listening to ourselves. As women, we've learned to put ourselves second or third. When we are children we express what we want and our wants are either negotiated or thwarted by our parents/caregivers who know what is best. Our agency is not fostered as young people. Toward the end of my marriage, I had the huge realization that I felt like I was riding side car in my husband's life. Somewhere along the line, I learned to arrive with the compromise instead of what I truly wanted. This is how I entered my conversations and conflict. I started the negotiations from a compromised point of view rather than from what I want. The ideas, thoughts, suggestions and feelings I proposed were not mine, they were what I thought he would agree to.

When I'm trying to prove myself, prove my credibility, prove that I belong somewhere or that I am good enough, what I'm really doing is trying to prove myself to myself. It is a matter of self-worth. The irony is that my judgment of my self-worth is really the only one that matters. I have to give myself permission to believe that my judgment of my self-worth is the only one that counts.

I was a really opinionated child and full of conviction. I had a lot of gumption to vocalize my thoughts. But, you get worn down. When I was young, my parents engineered my life for me. I didn't have agency in my nuclear family, so I tried to exercise it in my social circles. The result is that I got labeled as being really bossy. I remember being in an after school care program and the kids had elected someone to talk to me one day. The spokesperson said that they were not going to play with me anymore unless I stopped being bossy. I wasn't aware that I was bossy, so I was mortified and deeply hurt. I think it stung so badly because I wasn't aware. I just assumed people would speak up for themselves if they wanted or needed something, that they would be their own agent. I over corrected and was scared to be so forceful in the world because I was alienating people. I made myself small, quieter. I went into overcompensated negotiation. That kind of thing starts to rewire your brain. The thoughts you have become things, ways of being in real life. Now I realize it is not our job as women to make sure everyone feels ok. We're martyring ourselves to everyone else's comfort.

What It Means to Be a Woman

That's a messy question! It takes me in so many different directions at once. It's confusing. But I can't imagine the alternative! Women are so naturally powerful but by nature not prone to wield their power in the ways that we encounter power in our current world/culture. There is a dissonance when we come up against resistance, when we are pushed back or let down by current power-structures—even other women operating within these paradigms, which is somewhat even more disorganizing. The use of our power does not lend itself naturally to our solutions. Posturing with the power we are familiar with in these social structures feels disingenuous I think.

Feminine power has grace; it is both benevolent and awake. I know this, but have not yet fully experienced it. Knowing versus experiencing are radically different things. I am slowly learning to cultivate a space for myself and in my relationships with others that gives me the room to be authentically myself. Acceptance now has to come from within. As that starts to take a deeper hold, my potentials are felt. It is grounding, and then even a little mighty. I've been noticing I am coming into my body more. How was I walking around and accomplishing so much before while so disconnected?! My power is a tide of lost and found (and then lost again). I am okay with being lost for a time; I am not certain I have ever been truly 'found' (seen) and that has been a problem. Women are amazing.

What I Want to Get Out of Being a Woman

An immersive experience and radical acceptance: the courage for that to be true and the reasonable safety to explore all my options. The freedom to define myself as a human being. I am not a girl, I am a woman. I am not a mother, I am okay with that and I'm not selfish. I am not corporate, though I am ambitious and effective. I am not a prude, and not a slut, but I am sexual and adventurous and selective. I am not fragile, but I am vulnerable.

Something I Regret

Sharpshooter! Regret stings, but it is good to look at it, and feel your way through it. Learn, grow. Move to the next steps! I regret not going to France on summer exchange when I was turning 14. It was an opportunity to live with a French family for the summer to gain my fluency since my French grades had been so good. But something about it all scared me. I was unsettled and my parents dropped the issue quickly. In retrospect, I think my unsettled and scared feelings were a preconscious knowing that my family was disintegrating. My parents split months later, and my childhood ended abruptly from there. France might have opened a whole new way of being in the world, of seeing the world. The chance to plug into another family would have been invaluable in seeing myself, my family, and others in a way that challenged my unconscious filters and mindsets. A summer away would not have changed my parents divorcing, but it may have saved me from self-recruiting as my mother's (angry) guardian, and ultimately losing myself in a more dangerous world where I tried to escape into one of my heartfelt loves (horses), yet found myself sexually exploited by a father-like figure instead. Trust and self-worth were shattered by this domino of events, so my resilience built a fortress of walls that have been eclipsing my view for years, but these walls are now crashing down all around me.

The Legacy I Want to Live

Story + Wisdom + Courage = Self Love (and purpose). If I could do anything, anything, anything in this world, I would go get a Master of Fine Arts in documentary filmmaking. And I know the topic: it would be a documentary about being childless by choice. There is a deep misunderstanding and judgment from within and out associated with this, and so many stories to tell. Documentary is so powerful, so raw, so accessible and visual but it's the narrative that hits home; when the stories crawl under the skin and into the folds of our mind we are moved, changed and humbled a little bit more by shared, hopefully evolving, human experience. It would be my bliss to know how to start doing this.

Kate's international perspective caught me by surprise at first. "I never saw the limits of being a woman in the workplace until I moved to the States." Her statement reminded me of how important our stories are in shaping our culture, and how important our culture is in shaping our stories. What is culture other than a collective set of stories that are played out every day of our lives, moment to moment?

Listening to Kate makes me wonder how I can rewrite and recreate my story each day. Truth be told, when I think about changing my narratives I start to feel nervous. Let's say I wake up and decide that my new story is that I make equal pay to any male counterpart at a job. That could mean I need to ask for a raise, negotiate my benefits, and demand that I get paid what I am worth. What's more, it means that I may need to value myself, and stop worrying I might offend someone by asking for what I am worth. Re-writing our stories is a bold and courageous act. Kate reminds us that we have the power to create our own path.

KATE

Nottingham, England, 1963
Funny, lively, caring, authentic, sister, daughter, hard-working, bit wonky, a swimmer, loves to dance and do Zumba, career driven, American, English, serious, light-hearted, full of joy, a pioneer, eldest sister, wife, nature lover.

What I've Inherited

I was born in 1963, in my parent's bedroom, in their home in Nottingham, in the middle of England. I was my parents' first-born child, and I was a healthy bouncing baby girl with a shot of bright red hair, just like my paternal grandmother. I was born with that instant connection to my father's side of the family and that feeling of specialness to my father. As I found out later in life, I was my mother's second born child (as she had to give up her first born as she was an unmarried mother who got pregnant while training to be a nurse in London). Someone once said to me that as a result of this, I probably received the love of two children from her. She could not be with her first-born son to love him as she so wanted to, and they added that that is a lot to carry in my life. And that's how I still feel 51 years later: very special to my mother and father and so very, very loved. What a wonderful gift to receive; I am truly blessed.

My father's family name is Clifford, and they have lived and worked in Nottingham for many generations, going back as far as the 1700s. They were a family of miners, teachers, gypsies, engineers. My late uncle was the family historian and so I inherited a well-developed family tree. Granny Clifford was a lovely, warm-hearted, large lady who was widowed in her 50s (my grandfather dying early of lung cancer from his time as a miner). She was very shy and spent a lot of time alone after her

33

four children left home. The story goes that she once applied for a position and was rebuffed due to her 'station in life'—we now call this the working class she was born into—so she never tried to get work again. She accepted her lot, which is such a crappy British thing that still happens today, and in my family.

I love that I have inherited many wonderful characteristics from both of my parents:

From my father: my left-brain'ness, starting me in a career studying math and computing (my dad was an engineer), his very caring nature of family, his hard working nature, his sense of adventure and exploration, and his interest in we are what we eat and being healthy.

From my mother: her love of the outdoors, her dedication to doing great work in the community (volunteering and looking after the neighbors), her love of a good book and reading a lot, her caring nature (she was a nurse), her love and nurture of a great circle of friends, and her pioneering way of growing in her career and organizing and leading new initiatives.

What this all means is that I get to play in both the serious hard work of a business career and also bring in my deep caring of humans, nature, and animals. I can be deadly serious or I can be a goof ball - it all depends on the situation. As the eldest of 3, I was the only one to go to University and to live in another country. I accomplished many firsts for our family. My mother and father also did many new firsts in their family. I always felt this unwavering support to just be who I was meant to be, no pressure to do anything in particular, but to find my own way. Which I have done and continue to do!

An Inheritance I'd Like to Return

Sometimes, I still don't believe I can do things. This comes from the British culture and my family accepting their lot in life; I hear this all the time from my siblings. It holds me back and I think this is one of the reasons I love being in the US, where you can be what you want to be. My confidence holds me back, still today. I have done so many things and have pioneered my way through a tough career in computing and business—it feels embarrassing to write this.

What It Means to Be a Woman

I hate this question! I have always just been me. I studied math and computing, and I have worked in a male dominated field. I always felt I was always accepted just by being me. I never saw the limits of being a woman in the workplace, until I moved to the States and this became a label I had. I simply hate it. So I guess to be a woman means to be me! I have always been a tom boy in the way I look in my physical stature and dress. I think it's only recently that I have tapped into the more feminine caring side of me, from being at LIOS graduate school and having the time to spend with my family, neighbors and community.

As a side note, and one related to being a woman, I never wanted children. I knew this early on. This was particularly painful for me in my 30s as I prepared to get married for the first time and asked to be sterilized. The doctor refused saying this was not normal and that I needed to see a Psychologist, which I didn't. I was fuming. Having children pops up now and again, especially at this age (funnily enough). People who I don't know ask if I have children or assume I have them. Sometimes I feel a real freak saying, "No, I don't have children." This is weird to me, to be hitting this in my 40-50s.

What I Want to Get Out of Being a Woman

To rekindle the confidence to just be accepted for who I am; no labels, no judgment, or expectations.

Something I Regret

Not spending more happy time with my parents. I left home at 18 to go to University far away from my hometown. I spent years saying I never wanted to go back. My teenage years were very tough as Mum and Dad argued. The tension at home was awful. They got divorced in the first year I left home. This gave me the drive and energy to work hard in my career and life, but now I grieve for happy times with my folks. I have been working on this a lot over the last few years. I've had time to be with them in new ways and create new happy memories. These have been the most amazing times for me, and I want more. It's always in the back of my mind. Do I go back and live with my parents for a while? I would up and go if it was that simple, but it isn't. I have a new job, a great life, and my husband would not leave here. The best I can do is book lots of holiday time with them, but I am always wondering/dreaming about doing more. I think this is all about getting over my anger and disappointment of our family life in my teens. I love both of my parents, and getting divorced was the best thing for them. I have forgiven them for all the hard times as they were doing the best they could. I just want more family time with them.

The Legacy I Want to Live

That people see that you can make your own path, and be yourself, wherever you are. That people see my journey as a life well lived, and that I left an imprint on those I love. That people think of me with laughter and fondness.

I want other people to know it will be okay. Be yourself. It is okay to be yourself. A life well lived and an authentic life is more important than keeping up with the Joneses.

Katie's warm southern heart radiates with joy when she adventures to new cities and fosters community around her. She has a grounded presence rooted with elegance and femininity. Katie reveals the strength and agency of being a woman — the pleasure, responsibility, and confidence that comes from feeling capable and making your own decisions. With a tender honesty, she also reveals that though she is strong, she still craves to be loved and cared for. We are both independent and symbiotic.

After listening to the stories of Katie's beloved heirlooms, I reflected more on the exchange that occurs when passing on an inheritance. How do I become clearer on the inheritance I want to give? How do I return an inheritance I no longer want to keep? How do I choose who to offer my legacy to? Which bequests are the right and responsibility of an individual, and which are the right and responsibility of a collective?

KATIE

Knoxville, Tennessee, 1976

Sentimental, smart, southern, curvaceous, competitive, analytical, extroverted, social, lonely, astute observer of the world around me, a good friend, care taker, peace maker, send a lot out into the world but don't accept a lot back (but not because I don't want it), funny, reflective, I'm the decider, don't like when people are too cool for stuff, enjoy life, adventurous, up for fun and connection, ambitious, driven, good at what I do, I want to go places and do stuff.

What I've Inherited

From a tangible aspect, I've inherited a lot of our family's furniture, my grandmother's jewelry, and my mother's kitchen things. My mom passed away when I was 20. My dad, a couple years after my mother passed away, met another woman, married her, and they moved in together. He wasn't going to take the things they shared together to his new wife's house. So, I was able to take what I now consider heirlooms, but at the time were just her things—like the pots, pans, or the rocking chair that I was rocked in as a baby. I cook every day with the same pots and pans; I stir sauces with the same utensils that my mother did. I have many memories connected to her about meals we used to share together, or learning to cook, or being in the kitchen. When you look around my house there is stuff everywhere in every room from my family's house. I can walk from room to room and point to things that belonged to my family.

I guess what is sentimental to me is that it's been almost 20 years since I saw my mom, and these things are the reminders of the relationship I had with her. Even though they are just things, it makes me feel like I've assumed the role of custodian of her memory. I know that's not true, and it's kind of arrogant to say in some way, because my sister has memories of my mom. My brother, my dad, anybody that knew her has their own memories. But I feel like I've been asked to care for these objects that I'm certain have so much of her and my family soaked up into their cracks and crevasses. I'm protective of those things. It makes me feel connected to a past that I get further and further away from all the time.

Sometimes I think of myself as a very, very womanly woman. Everything about my physical countenance is super womanly. There's not a straight line on my body. I am a very warm and openhearted person, which is something I associate a lot with femininity. I'm a nurturer and a caretaker in ways I think are very womanly. I've inherited the shape of my body from my family. I'm a pretty curvaceous lady. I have really big boobs and a great big ass. I wear an insane bra size. I have to buy my bras from specialty bra shops, because you can't just walk into Nordstrom and find a really nice-looking 32 E bra. And if you do find them they're going to look like shields. In some ways that's one of my favorite parts of my body. I think I have a very nice bust line. But, I lost my mom and her mom both to breast cancer. It's really scary thinking about that. I worry—will they turn on me? Will I have problems related to my health in the future? I have a love/hate relationship with them.

What I Want to Get Out of Being a Woman

I don't always think of myself as being a woman. Then I have to remind myself that I'm 37 years old and I am a grown-ass woman. I don't have a lot of the trappings of middle age—like I don't have a husband or children. I'm not responsible for picking people up at carpool or the stuff I associate with full-on womanhood. When I was growing up that is what the women in my life did.

When I think of what it's like being a woman, it's about owning the entitlement and the responsibility of adulthood. Owning that you're a grown-ass woman that makes her own decisions and advocates for herself. You can do whatever you want. You are the decider, you are the one who will make yourself thrive or not thrive, or pursue the things you want or not. It's all up to you. There's not another person who will say, "Well you should really think about what happens with your children and save your money." I'm the only one who is going to say yes or no, and that's great.

But, it's also like, 'I'm the only person who is holding myself back.'

I've been alone in my life as an adult for so long that I've taken on a lot of responsibility. I just do everything for myself because there is no one else around to do it. I open my own doors, carry my own bags, pay my own bills or my taxes, or get an oil change. All the details of my life I manage all myself. Sometimes when I interact with women who are coupled they abdicate a lot of responsibility to their partners in ways that don't occur to me. Several years ago I went to go have a weekend at a beach house with a friend and her husband. When I arrived, my friend told her husband to go get my bag. It was super nice but I was like, "You don't have to do that. I can carry my own bag." I wasn't expecting anybody to take care of that shit for me. I wouldn't have asked anyone to do that. Her husband grabbed the keys and went out to get my bags from the car and I started to cry. It never would have occurred to me to ask. No one takes care of me like that. In some ways I wish someone did, because I've done all those things for myself for so long it is hard for me to be vulnerable and let others take care of me. That is a weird part of being the woman that I am. I am okay being very open-hearted and being very generous with emotion, but because I've been doing things for myself for so long I have a hard time letting others do things for me.

I was a third wheel on a date the other night. My friend expressed the desire for popcorn but it wasn't ready yet and the popcorn lady said to come back in 10 minutes. We got our seats, and my friend's boyfriend popped up probably exactly 10 minutes after we sat down. He ran out and got popcorn. He wanted to retrieve the thing that my friend wanted. To go get the thing that would make her happy. I was like, 'yeah man, way to step up and get the popcorn!' I was really happy for my friend, but a tiny part of me thought if I wanted popcorn, I would have to go get my own-ass popcorn.

And that's fine. It's not a burden to go get my own popcorn, but it was a reminder that anything that I want or that I'm going to have, I'm going to do for myself. Not because I'm determined to do it for myself, but because it is out of necessity. If I want popcorn, I need to march my happy ass up to the counter and get my own damn popcorn. There's not going to be someone who says, "Katie, I'll get your popcorn, let me do that for you." And sometimes, I want somebody to get me popcorn. I don't think there is anyone who wants to make me happy right now. I mean, my parents want to take care of me and my family loves me. My friends have a genuine interest in my happiness. There's just not someone out there dreaming up ways to make me smile. If I were in a relationship I know I would be thinking that way. I'd be thinking, 'This person likes this kind of soda so I'm going to stock it even though I don't think it is good at all. I am going to keep it in my refrigerator so when they come over they would have their favorite soda.'

The Legacy I Want to Live

The first thing that came to mind when you asked what I want to pass on was, 'To whom? To children that I may or may not have?' I don't know if I'll ever be a mom. What is weird is that I actually think I would be a really great mother. I don't know if I want the opportunity to pursue motherhood without a partner. I'm not ready to change my whole life to be a single parent. That's not really part of my dream. That wouldn't be the best situation for me to be the best version of a mother I can be. I've got real high standards for what that would be. I'd want to do it in a way that I could be a great parent instead of somebody who is barely making it.

I would want to leave a legacy of inspiration and friendship. I'd love to say that I'd been a really good friend, and that I inspired people to contribute in their own lives in a meaningful and authentic way. I struggle with that too—am I contributing enough? Is the world I live in right now affording me enough opportunities to impact people's lives? How will I be remembered? Would I even be remembered? I think about that sometimes and it stresses me out. Are people going to say that she was a really good leadership development professional? Or are they going to say she was a really good friend? Or she was a kind neighbor? Or she kept the house pretty clean? Or she could really sing? I don't know. I feel a lot of pressure to leave a legacy of something grand, and I don't know that I have yet. I want to know that I will. Or that what I'm doing right now with my time is enough.

Katy is the older sister of my childhood best friend. Though it has been over 20 years since Katy and I actually spoke, she was profoundly honest and vulnerable sharing her story. I deeply admire this quality in Katy. She openly offers the richness and integrity of her soul. She raises important questions: how do you start feeling worthy of getting the things you want? How do you let go of who you want to be and accept who you are? How do you identify your own voice amidst all the noise? Will you let others hear your story, and how will you deal with their reaction?

One of the last things Katy said to me in the interview was, "Be inspired to own your story and heal. I would love to see that, I would love to have that." I would love that too.

KATY

Washington, D.C., 1980
Passionate, bibliophile, introverted, intense, confused, molder of minds, protector of children, difficult, perfectionist, athletic, outspoken, opinionated, Army brat, recovering Catholic, independent, stubborn, music lover (especially old jazz on vinyl!), tree hugger, subsistence lifestyle liver, adventure lover, sassy, sarcastic, unforgiving.

What I've Inherited

From my mother, I inherited this fabulously thick, curly, red mane that makes up its own mind about how it will look, despite any products I slather it in. There are not enough pins or elastics in the world to restrain my mane and I love it that way. Sometimes it drives me absolutely insane, but it has become a majorly defining trait in my life. I really feel that my hair parallels my character in every way.

When I was young, my hair was stick straight. I always admired my mother's gorgeous hair and was envious of her curls. When my older brother graduated from high school, he quit cutting his hair and I quickly became jealous of the untamable red curls he grew. It seemed so unfair to me that a man should be gifted with the hair I so desperately wanted— fun, vivacious, unique, attention-grabbing hair that screams at the world, "I am *awesome!*"

Desperate to rid myself of the nerdy, painfully shy impression I made with my long, straight hair and big, plastic glasses, I did everything I could to curl my hair, from sleeping on old-fashioned sponge rollers to horrific chemical perms. But nothing ever got me the curls I so badly wanted. I finally accepted defeat and gave up trying to make my mane something it wasn't (much like my below-average breasts) when a miracle occurred. I woke up one morning during my second year of college and went through my normal shower-and-go routine. I was slouched over the breakfast table when my roommate came into the kitchen and queried, "You curled your hair?!?" She was flabbergasted, knowing how little time I actually invested in my hair. I was shocked and, having no idea what she was talking about, darted into the bathroom to look in the mirror. Lo and behold, my hair had dried curly! I was totally ecstatic—I finally had the mane I wanted, and it's stayed that way for the last fifteen years. (I joke that the literally overnight change from straight to kinky was the end of puberty for me. I never got the big boobs I wanted, but I am totally in love with my hair.) I've since shaved my head twice and got my curls back both times. They make me stand out in a crowd; add a sassiness to my appearance that I feel is a truer representation of my character than my stick straight locks were. The painfully shy, nerdy girl I was grew into a sassy, confident, fun woman and I'm grateful to have hair that reflects that.

An Inheritance I'd Like to Return

Ugh, this question is hard. The last several months I've reflected on so much that I've inherited that disgusts me. I have a sharp tongue. I'm quick to lash out. I'm slow to forgive. I hate, hate, *hate* to feel emotionally vulnerable, even (and maybe especially) around my husband. But I think the thing I hate most that I inherited, or maybe learned, is feeling guilty all the time. I feel guilty about living a life that makes me happy because it keeps me so far away from my family. I feel guilty if I don't call my parents once a week, even though they literally never call me, not even on my birthday. I feel guilty if I don't make time to fly to their home in the Lower 48 to visit, even though they've never been to visit me. I feel guilty if I go to visit my husband's family because my mother is jealous of the healthy relationship I have with my in-laws. I feel guilty that I have a better relationship with my in-laws than I do with my own family. I feel guilty if I say no to extra duties at work. I feel guilty if I say no to extra duties with my rowing club. I feel guilty if I choose something that's in my own best interest if it means not helping someone else. I feel guilty about sometimes just needing to stay home and be quiet and not going out to socialize. I feel guilty about spending money, about not spending money, about not being more helpful on our house projects, and about sleeping in late. I am overwhelmed with guilt about the choices I make. If I walk by a piece of trash on the beach and don't pick it up, I will agonize about it afterward, feeling awful about not doing my part to care for our earth when someone else so clearly hasn't done theirs. I won't take the last piece of anything edible at social functions because I will feel badly about it. Sometimes, I can't even make decisions because I am paralyzed by making the RIGHT one (whatever THAT means) and the impact it will have.

I know, after hours and hours of therapy, that my mother wields guilt as a weapon the way a judge wields justice. She is so damned good at it that even a tone of voice can make me feel lower than dirt. If I call on a weekday rather than a weekend, she will answer the phone with, "What's wrong? It's the middle of Friday afternoon." And her tone is not laced with concern; it's accusatory, as though I've interrupted her, inconvenienced her, annoyed her and it's made her angry. I have so internalized the guilt that my mother uses to manipulate us that I can't make even simple decisions. When my husband and I go to town (Anchorage), we have the same conversation about where to eat. I know, and he knows, that I really want to eat Asian food, every time. But he doesn't. So we go around and around because I don't want him to eat something he doesn't want to eat, but I'm also afraid to just say what I want. And I don't just do that with my husband. I am a classic deflector. Someone says to me, "What do you want [fill in the blank—to do, to eat, to see at the theater, etc.]?" my automatic response is, "I don't know, what do you want?" Even if I know there's something I really, really want, I will always feel out the other person or people because I'm afraid of wanting the wrong thing or suggesting the wrong thing. I know that I will feel badly—guilty—for not being in the same mindset as the present company. And it drives me crazy.

I want desperately to have children, but we've been having a hard time. We're about to embark on a journey of diagnosis and who-knows-what to try to conceive. But I am terrified of having children. I am scared shitless that I will become her, and that they will become me. I don't ever, EVER want my child to sit in some man or woman's office in tears because I have unintentionally laid so much guilt on their narrow shoulders that they can't even tell someone what they want for dinner. I don't ever want my child to feel guilty rather than loved. And of course, I feel guilty writing that down, for speaking ill of my mother.

What It Means to Be a Woman

Being a woman is complicated, isn't it? I want to be respected for my brain, but also be desired for my body. If someone catcalls at me while I am running down the road, or says something lewd to me in a bar, I am outwardly offended and secretly thrilled. How dare someone treat me with such vulgarity, as if I am a piece of meat? And yet, I also feel flattered and empowered that someone felt so affected by my looks that they had to act, even in an offensive way. It's so strange. In most situations, I feel fabulous when someone compliments an idea I've shared, or agrees that my thoughts are spot-on. But I want the whole shebang—I want to be admired as smart *and* beautiful, intelligent *and* sexy. To me, that's the difficulty about being a woman: it's never enough. Women have, for so long, been valued for their domesticity, for their bodies, and for their baby making. But we've been demanding more for a long time now. Being a woman right now means we're caught somewhere in the middle: we're expected to be nurturing, strong, caring, hold a job and put a meal on the table. In our efforts towards equality, we've wound up just taking on more of the work. I feel like women bear so much more of the burden of our society than do the men, though I can't really know that, since I'm not a man. I don't know if women are more emotionally complex than men, but I know that we seem to have a way of using emotions to complicate even simple situations.

Women have worked themselves into a place that's never enough. If you're a stay-at-home mom, you're less than whole and less valuable to society because you don't have a job. I've seen some fabulous moms who are constantly explaining, sometimes defensively, that they USED to work and will work again when their kids go to school. I definitely want to have a family, but I'm also afraid of giving up my career. If you have a job and no children (like me), you're also less than whole. In my position as a teacher, parents sometimes tell me I can't understand something because I haven't reproduced. So the value that I hold—intellectually, emotionally, the role I play in guiding their children, protecting them, nurturing them, educating them—is diminished because of my reproductive status.

To me, that statement perfectly sums up what being a woman is now: it's a struggle. It is a struggle to be valued for exactly the person you are at exactly that moment, not the person you were or the person you will be.

What I Want to Get Out of Being a Woman

I just want to be happy. I want to live to a ripe old age with my husband, fill my life with adventure, and work with children, empowering them all—girls and boys alike— to mold this world into one where equality is valued over everything else, where they speak up for themselves, each other, and for the Earth.

Something I Regret

I am fiercely independent, often to a fault. When I moved to bush Alaska all by myself, I thought I was going to live this life where I could just be me, take care of myself, and feel good about it. But I very quickly learned that no one, no matter their skill set, can make it alone in remote Alaska. We all need each other here. Learning to ask for help over these last eight years has been incredibly difficult for me—possibly the most difficult thing I've had to learn, ever. Even growing up, I didn't ask for help. My siblings were all very needy and demanding of my parents' attention, frequently acting out in inappropriate ways, getting in trouble with police, partying hard and so on. My younger sister is very manipulative and has some pretty serious alcohol and drug addiction issues. She has my parents both wrapped so tightly around her fingers that they will literally drop everything and drive for days to come to her rescue.

Somewhere in all of that, I decided that the way to earn my parents' love and affection was to play by the rules, live up to my potential, do what was expected of me. So I did—honor roll, honors classes, first chair saxophone, varsity athlete in multiple sports, yearbook editor, etc., etc. I never drank in high school, never tangled with the cops, never had sex, never so much as smoked a cigarette. I did what I could to be the model child, a responsible human being that my parents could rely on and be proud of—classic middle child. I learned to be totally independent so that my parents wouldn't ever have to worry about me. I became a college athlete, veered off the straight and narrow a bit, but always kept my goals in mind and made a point of never needing to call home to ask for help, even if I really did need it.

Now, at 34 years old, I'm realizing how much damage my fierce independence has done to my relationship with my parents. When I was young, my parents had so much on their plates with my siblings' shenanigans that there just wasn't enough time for me. My being so good meant they didn't put much effort into me (or so it felt, and still does when I reflect on it). This has carried over into my adult life. I've established my life here in Alaska, chosen this place to make my home. My parents have never been to visit, not once in eight years. My parents, who travel to my sister's home—wherever it is—twice a year, can't seem to find the time, money, desire to visit me. My parents have, in essence, rejected me. They can't understand my life here, don't express any interest in understanding my life, my husband, or my love affair with Alaska. They don't call me; I'm not even sure if they know my phone number. And when I confronted my mother about it a few months ago, she said to me, "Well, you never needed me. You just didn't have room in your life for me." So my attempts to make her life easier by being a model child have resulted in my not having a mother, not the way my girlfriends do. And certainly not the way my sister does, my sister who seems to have a monopoly on my mother's time, love, affection, concern and interest.

I guess all of this is a long-winded way of saying that my sense of independence on which I so pride myself, my ability to stand on my own two feet, also brings me heartbreak. That independence is something I inherited, something I built on as a teenager, developing it into one of my strongest traits. Now it's the downfall of my relationship with my mother and sometimes causes conflict with my husband. I both love my independence and resent it. I resent needing to care for myself because my siblings needed so damned much. But I'm grateful as hell to not have ever found myself in any of the messes they did. It's a terrible paradox.

The Legacy I Want to Live

I want to pass on a legacy of love. When I die, I want people to comment on how much I loved—them, my students, the world, adventure. I want folks to talk about how hard I worked with my students, how hard I push them to be the best "them" they can be, especially the ones from damaged homes. I want folks to talk about the crazy things I did—traveling around Africa, hiking Kilimanjaro, moving to remote Alaska, learning to fish, to hunt, to eat crazy food. I want folks to remember how much I love my husband, how hard I work to be a good wife to him. I want folks to remember my quick wit, my sassiness, my intelligence. When folks bring up my name after I die, I want them to laugh and feel loved.

Kelly has a tender and wild femininity that surges through her. It is the graceful rush of life force itself. From Kelly, and from many of the other women I interviewed, one of the consistent themes I heard was the paradox of wholeness. Women want to be seen as being multi-dimensional and yet we burn ourselves out trying to be everything to everyone. How can we possibly be graceful, awkward, wild, domestic, organized, and spontaneous all at once? We struggle tirelessly to be enough, but not too much. We go to great lengths to hide or fix the pieces we deem ugly or broken. Despite the relentless efforts to wear masks of perfection, I believe women genuinely want to be seen for all their pieces, to be seen as whole.

There is so much fear being a woman: fear of not being heard, not being seen, and not being loved. What would happen if women were no longer afraid? At one point or another we've all transformed fear into action, fear into success, or fear in to love. What must happen to turn the fear of being a woman into greatness? What must happen to turn the fear of being ME into love?

KELLY

Albuquerque, New Mexico, 1979
Adaptable, whole-hearted, intuitive, empathic, weird, adventurous, sensitive, curious, opinionated, conscientious, genuine, sociable, kinesthetic, affectionate, creative, natural, playful, optimistic, coordinated, dreamy.

What I've Inherited

My mom and I were both laughing about something the other day. It was small and silly, tears rolling down our faces. It's rarely ever a dry eye, even when we smile. The women in my family tear up easily. It's an uncontrollable release that for some reason flows whether we are happy, sad, disappointed, or embarrassed. Laughing is like a water geyser exploded. I love my laugh. It is an uninhibited burst of emotion, and the tears flow like the river wild. I get lots of compliments on my laugh, and the tear factor seems to impress, amaze, and endear people. Sometimes my tears are misinterpreted. Genetically, I think we have really active tear ducts, and more true, we are easily amused by the world, which is something that I love and embrace about this trait. We recognize that life isn't always easy or pleasant. We have a knack for recognizing absurdities, the weirdness in life, and be able to enjoy a good laugh. I personally am drawn to people, experiences, and professions that are emotive, expressive, and animated over sterile, controlled, and uptight. We do have that gregarious Irish blood in us after all. We don't laugh just to laugh, but when we do, it is an experience.

What It Means to Be a Woman

My mind juts off in many directions with this question. First, I think about all the things that women are told overtly or subliminally that they can and can't do. And time and time again, women are breaking records, defying odds, running companies, flying planes, raising kids on their own, surviving abuse, rising above, and risking their lives for freedom. Women define and exemplify that what seems impossible, out of reach, highly unlikely, and never been done before—possible, real, brought to light, birthed, uncovered, alive, and connected.

What I Want to Get Out of Being a Woman

There are some things I get out of being a woman that I love, and some things that I don't. Even though I do not want to have children personally, I love the fact that a woman's body is the resting and nurturing place for human life, and the portal to which all human life enters the world. That is pretty darn special! I enjoy wearing make-up, and jewelry, and all the different style options on the clothes spectrum we can rock from pants, skirts, heels, flats—you name it. I love the anatomy of a woman. I love the qualities that are typically innate to women: intuitive, nurturing, community-minded, connectors, etc.

What I also get from being a woman, but don't like, is that it now has become necessary for a woman to be escorted down streets, to her car, or up to her front door. I'm not talking about gestures that are intended to be kind and chivalrous. I don't like that this is more about feeling safe or protecting a woman from possible attack. There is a lot of fear that comes with being a woman that I wish were different. And I'm uncertain how to change this.

The Legacy I Want to Live

This topic, the legacy of women, is really alive. It immediately resonated; I am honored to be a part of it. So many different streams of thought were ignited by these questions. There were 5-10 ways I could have answered each of the questions. I felt like I wanted a balance of stories—some that felt more heavy, and others that were more light in their energy. I appreciate both aspects and didn't want my chapter to be focused on only one thing or another. There are stories from long ago that continue to play out in my life today. I really want to capture the wholeness of my story rather than only particular scenes. For example: The kid thing came up. How can you be an ambassador of legacy without kids? Body image? What are the benefits to being a woman? What comes with being a woman that I don't have control over (the positive and negative)? Safety things came up a lot. It is more acceptable for a woman to show affection to children. What about transgendered people?

I wish to pass on a legacy of practicing genuine presence with ourselves and with others. I believe being present to our experiences is how we learn about ourselves, our world, and each other. I hope to pass on the knowing that each of us is significant beyond measure; that our purpose doesn't lie in our job, possessions, or achievements, but rather in the being-ness and expression of our authentic song.

I have been on that soapbox lately. It's been really alive for me in the past 8-9 years. Before, I would feel a lot of anxiety about what I was supposed to do and pressure to be at a certain place in my life. I became more and more stressed out and worried. There was a lot shaming and blaming. 'You don't have your shit together; you need to get your shit together.' I felt like I was fighting my natural intuitive instincts. The linear path didn't resonate with my spirit at all. The path is more windy.

The last few years I stopped thinking about my purpose as my career and my job—it's so much more than that. I felt was a sigh of relief. People create this connection with their job and career and how they define themselves. Their definition of success is in that role, in how they make their living. I really don't like to use my job to define myself.

When you meet someone, one of the first questions asked is "What do you do?" I feel a shield put up when people hit you with their rehearsed elevator speech. It's cold. It's a barrier between me and the other person. But, I can see the value in each person. I know there is so much more to this person than this elevator speech (not to disregard their achievements). Instead, ask 'how do you like to spend your time, what inspires you, what kinds of things are you passionate about?' Think about how can you describe yourself and what you do in a way that resonates with you – not just how it fits into an elevator speech template? What are you using to define yourself? What if we lost the elevator speech culture and traded it in for a more authentic conversation? What if we talked about our highest excitement? Change the question and see how it changes the conversation.

This is something I've gone rouge with in my family. The family story is to take the most linear path, the one that is most safe—the corporation path. None of the women in my family have an entrepreneurial tendency. The corporate path didn't resonate for me and I had to convince myself to venture out on my own, to be in business for myself. It was a significant rewriting of story, from 'corporate path' to 'I can rely on myself and do things differently.' I think these are messages that are more characteristic for a man. The linear path story has been a straitjacket I've had to wiggle out of. It's a straitjacket that has been passed on from generation to generation. It might have suited one person at one time. There might be guilt that if you don't do it you'll disappoint everyone. The loyalty to the story and to my family is confining and restrictive. They are hard patterns to break.

I think right now, in society, women are trying to break out of the straitjacket too. They are ready to say, "No, I'm not going to wear this jacket!" It is the most frustrating feeling to be confined by someone else who has no business even suggesting you wear this jacket. This is where the irate anger and rage come from. Restrictions on women's healthcare and reproductive health, for example. People make decisions, but have no business having a conversation about that, about ME.

The first time I met Nicole, I was auditioning to be an intern with Sinner Saint Burlesque. She was a local comedian and the MC at that time. Nicole raises questions for me that I know frustrate many women: how do I do it all? How do I have it all? How do I be it all? On the days I get stuck trying to do it all, Nicole inspires me to flip my thinking and ask myself these questions: why do I think I have to do it all? Who is telling me to be it all? What do I want for myself (rather than how do I satisfy everyone else)?

NICOLE

Dearborn, Michigan, 1980
Excitable, funny, grumpy, moody, cheap, poor, thrifty, voluptuous, vivacious, smart, articulate, quick, sickly, drunk, thick, loud, sexy, anxious, giving, rebel.

What I've Inherited

My grandparents just loved me a whole lot. I'd spend summers with them. I was super close to my maternal grandmother. She would always leave the house with earrings on. She taught me manners, about going out to eat, how to put on deodorant, and things like that. I felt like I didn't get the end of the lessons on how to be a lady, because she died when I was 13.

I'm always happy that I got my body-type from my grandmother. She assured me once when I was very young that, despite being big, I would be very well proportioned. It was hard when I was younger, but now that I'm an adult being a larger person has gotten easier. Plus, I don't always have to stand in the back of group photos, now that most other people have caught up in size.

My grandmother was an early feminist. I'm glad she passed that on to me. I have a photo of her and I when I was a baby. She was wearing a shirt that read "Never underestimate the power of a woman." I always thought that was such a great role model.

My grandmother was unusually tall, not like side show, but like 6 feet tall. This was unusual, especially in her generation. She always came from this place of power. She was man-sized. There is nothing a man could do that she couldn't. If anyone wanted to bother her, it was like, 'Really, what are you going to do?' She was pretty dominant in her marriage. It was not really an equal partnership. I think this might be because her father wasn't around when she was growing up. Whereas in most friends' homes you'd wait till the dad got home for a decision, that didn't happen in her home. As a result, she may have just thought, 'Why would any man tell me what to do?' Women in my family are in charge. Both my mother and grandmother were in charge.

An Inheritance I'd Like to Return

The hardest part was thinking about what I wish I hadn't inherited. I didn't want to find fault in my mother, but I got things I wish I didn't.

My mom is so butch, not very girly. She's like, "We don't need all that bullshit—all we need is our Miller Light and tiny cigars." For my wedding my mom brought her own 12 pack of Miller Lite. I was like, "Did you seriously bring cans of Miller Lite to my wedding?" In every picture she's holding one. My parents are both a hoot and love to party, and good people but sometimes I'm like, 'What are you doing!?'

She had low self-esteem that rubbed off on me. The cornerstone of this is that I feel like I look trashy; that people can see poorness on me. I feel like even if I was stark naked, people could still read it on me.

I was applying for my first job when I was about 15 and I remember my mom telling me that there are certain kinds of jobs people like me don't get. She told me I could never be a receptionist 'cause I'm not pretty enough. She said, "It's not that you aren't pretty, it's just that you're not pretty in that way. You don't have what it takes to work in offices." She never told me I was ugly. My sister told me I'd achieved being able to look like a lady more than anyone else in the family. She said I'd figured out how to be glamorous. I never thought of that as a skill set. Doing burlesque introduced me to that, though. Maybe no one ever told my mom how to clean up.

My mom has hated everything about her looks from as far back as I could remember. She once told me that good things don't happen to people that look like us. That has always stuck with me. There is always this feeling in the back of my head that when something goes poorly it's because of my looks. I don't think I'm ugly, but I worry that my appearance is low class. I have a hard time dressing up in things other than costumes. Every time I go for a job interview I end up looking like a mail order bride.

What It Means to Be a Woman

STRESS! I think being a woman in the modern world is incredibly stressful. I find that, despite having the same work load, I take on the lion's share of responsibilities around the house.

I think that more than ever women are being pulled in so many directions in popular culture. I struggle with the questions of whether to enhance my appearance with beauty products to presumably help me get ahead, or to shun notions like that completely and go all "Earth-mother" with it. Every time I shave I have an existential crisis!

When I think of being a woman, I imagine an image of a swirly lady cradling a baby. I don't feel like that at all most of the time. I feel pulled in a million directions. The modern woman is not only smart but also fun and educated and beautiful and sexy and you have to be all these things at once to be the top dog. It's a lot of pressure. There are times I feel beautiful, times I feel smart—they are all at different times. How do I pull all those things together?! There are days when I have shiny, bouncy hair, but my grammar is terrible. Sometimes I devote myself to intellectual pursuits and other times I'm in my yoga pants listening to jazz music and I kind of stink. Other times I'm wearing the right underwear and my eyelashes are great (ye-ah, I bought these!), but I don't want to do my math. We are supposed to be all those things, and we're supposed to give the impression we're all those things. It scares me to have to try to do everything at the same time. How do I be in front of people and be put together and knowing what I talking about?! What do I do when I can't fall back on self-deprecation when things aren't going well?

What I Want to Get Out of Being a Woman

Besides the free drinks!? I want to be able to help people. I don't think that requires being a woman but since I don't want children, I guess I just want to help everyone else in some way.

Something I Regret

I wish I hadn't waited so long to come out of my shell as an adult. I was crippled by shyness well into my late 20's. It wasn't until I started doing comedy at 27 that I was even able to talk to people. Had I known that people might actually like me when I was younger it might have made my early adult years better. Of course, having all that alone time is probably why I developed a sense of humor and a quick wit.

The Legacy I Want to Live

I don't want kids. I've held a baby one time in my life and I've never baby sat because I was 10 years younger than anyone else in my family. I see kids, and they are kinda dirty. I do have the need to pass on my wisdom. When I do shows it's a way to pass on the things I think are necessary to pass on on-stage.

I want future generations to know that you don't have to be born into money or have great looks to do something in the world. Most of my old teachers would have pegged me as a drop-out risk or a criminal when I was a kid. I always knew that wasn't me, but it took a lot of work to prove it to other people. I still feel like I'm proving it all the time. (In retrospect I maybe should have considered the neck tattoos a little harder.) Nevertheless, I want to teach others that being low class doesn't have to mean you don't have class. It just means you don't have any money. I also want people to see behind the veil. What is behind what is being sold to people? Think critically. Don't believe anyone—think about their motivation.

Kate is going to turn the world inside out by writing a book that will revolutionize the way people feel about their bodies. She told me, "I have yet to meet someone whose mother and father modeled what it looked like to actively love themselves—I want my children to know what it looks like to be in relationship with yourself, relationship with another, and to work for love." After talking with Kate I asked myself three important questions: if I fully loved and accepted myself, what would I stop doing every day? What would I start doing every day? What could I do with all the extra time I've gained from not trying to fix myself anymore?! Following those questions, I wondered if I could rally the courage to ask myself for forgiveness for 33 years of criticizing myself. And could I accept my own apology? Kate challenges me to practice self-love…and to start doing it right now.

KATE

Boulder, Colorado, 1985

Authentic, upbeat, positive, funny, joyful, mature, present, self-critical, balanced, anxious, light-hearted, energized, centered, hesitant, trusting, solid, trustworthy, stable, open, shy, steady, so many beautiful contradictions, feeling pretty whole right now. When I wrote twenty things about me, I was struck by the fact that I was like a walking contradiction. I could hold the dichotomy between who I am and where my value system lies, and where I want to be. I felt all at once stable and adventurous. For one of the first times in my life I felt comfortable holding the polarities inside of myself—that I could be messy and clean at the same time. That has really stayed in my psyche.

What I've Inherited

While it took a really long time for me to come to love them, I love my breasts, inherited from my paternal grandmother. I think that the reason that I love them is *because* they took so long to learn to love. I began developing early, when I was in elementary school. My relationship with my body—which had once been natural, aligned, and unconscious—became awkward and uncomfortable. All of a sudden, I began attracting attention from guys. Things that once were easy became more difficult with the pubescent transformation, and I remember dressing in baggier clothes and curling my shoulders to hide my chest.

I was 10. We were at the beach, and I vividly remember this. My bathing suit had a bow on it. I was there with my older cousin who was 11. Boys start making fun of me and pushing me. I thought they were flirting with my cousin. Then one boy asked me for my number. All of a sudden, I realized my body was something to be looked at. It had never occurred to me. That was when my emotional relationship with my body began. I was curvaceous through high school. I was known as the girl with the big boobs from my friends. In college I went on birth control pills, which made my breasts grow. The change caused me to suddenly need to re-familiarize myself with my body.

It wasn't until college that I began to realize I did not need to be ashamed of something that just came with this body—the same body that gives me so many other gifts. I was part of a conservative Christian community. Anything smelling of sexuality was not welcome. There were these things on my chest that would continue to grow. I couldn't recognize them as a part of me, especially as a beautiful part of me, because they were seen as something sexual. I began trying to physically avert attention to them and cover them up. When I started to free myself spiritually I began to have a relationship with my body, and breasts in particular. I didn't have to feel awkward or shy or shameful. They didn't have to be sexual, they could just be me. Previously, the only time I could physically be free and appreciate my breasts would be in marriage. But now, I could have a relationship with my body without being married. I worked very hard for that, not being awkward. Now I think they are pretty fucking phenomenal. My breasts are a celebration of my womanhood, a physical example of learning how to love my body, and my new favorite inheritance. They are something special, and everyone's are something special. Transformative shit.

What It Means to Be a Woman

For me, to be a woman means strength, power, grace, and warmth. To be a woman means to be strong and powerful like a river is strong and powerful, flowing and constant. To be a woman means the marriage of strength, softness, authentic love and genuine warmth. To be a woman means the intimate power of influence. It means sensuality, and waves of emotion. In our world, to be a woman means to be feared.

What I Want to Get Out of Being a Woman

I am writing a book on body love. My work in writing this book has revealed to me the pieces of every woman's story I connect with. When I interview women, all of a sudden I am intimately connected with their story. I begin to know them, to see them and to briefly become them.

I want to be able to embrace my femininity. I want to be able to use the unique qualities of being a woman to change the world, to create freedom, and, someday, to raise children who are free. I want goddess-like feminine power and feminine sexuality. I want the combination of strength and power, grace and warmth, and nurture and fierceness. This is an incredibly powerful thing, and I think most of the world is afraid of it. I have been afraid to be vocal and afraid to be powerful. I have been afraid to be that fierce chick that I want to be. That's the piece of my femininity I want to step into.

I had a conversation with my mother about why I left the church. (I'm also shacking up with my boyfriend now, god forbid.) The church had been a huge part of my life. I realized I was giving up part of myself to fit in to the church. Part of the reason I stayed with the church so long, was that I was given black or white instructions. When things are black and white, it's easy to stay in the lines. When I started messing with the gray, it got confusing and I started thinking.

As I began working with a therapist, she gave me permission to not be who I had always been. I met people with different world views and different experiences. With every conversation my comfort zone widened. Out of all my values, one of my highest values is compassion. I witnessed compassion outside of the church, which was where I had always experienced it. This was so freeing for me. I loved the idea of living a wide life and having a diverse community. New friends helped me see all the manifestations of authenticity—what a wonderful thing, to witness that. The more I see people be real with themselves, the more it has given me permission to be real with myself. You can be authentically you, and I can be authentically me. There doesn't have to be a compromise between holding multiple authenticities. When I help raise the next generation, I hope to raise them with the permission to be themselves. I want to pass on that there are different manifestations of a beautiful soul and each soul should be able to do its soul's work.

Something I Regret

My biggest regret is the fact that, when I was a youth minister, I taught the women in the youth group—not in words, but in underlying message—

that their bodies should be hidden; that their bodies could lead to sin; that they were responsible for protecting men from temptation. Now that I've allowed myself the freedom to love my body, explore my sexuality and sensuality, and be fully loved, I recognize how contained I allowed myself, my strength, and my power to become.

The Legacy I Want to Live

I want to pass on love. Self-love. Compassion. I want to pass on what it looks like to fully model love for another and love for self. I want to model for my children what it looks like to love and be loved. I have yet to meet someone whose mother and father modeled what it looked like to actively love themselves—I want my children to know what it looks like to be in relationship with yourself, relationship with another, and to work for love.

Women need to unleash themselves, release themselves. I think there are very few truly shitty people in the world and the rest is all just brokenness. Women are waiting, and they just need someone to say, "You don't have to be this." You can unleash yourself. You can choose.

CAT

San Francisco, California, 1981
Feminist, performer, graceful, tenacious, curious, leading thinker, world traveler, guarded, idealistic, re-wilding, psychic, poised, responsible, dream big, learner, 'well behaved women seldom make history.'

What I've Inherited

I am from a family of healers, teachers, and warriors. My blood pulses with wanderlust, a desire to help others restore their joy, and the rallying cry to promote social justice. I revel in the opportunity to rise to an occasion, to seek glory, and to find new ways of understanding the world. I am still recovering from the trauma and grief of being a rootless military child, though I am able to savor the global perspective, resilience, and social skills I gained. Living in a militaristic and patriarchal world taught me a great deal about rank, power and authority, as well as sacrifice, service and strength. I've spent many of my adult years learning healthier ways to exemplify these qualities.

I've inherited a high sensitivity to emotion and intuition, something each of my immediate family members has. This allows me to attune quickly to the energy of others, for better or for worse. I am grateful that my mother modeled being intuitive. I cannot imagine living life without my intuition and sense of spiritual connection.

My Nonna was a seamstress, and a popular one at that. She frequently told me how she made winter coats for the Kennedys. Every Saturday night was dance party night. My sisters and I would rummage through her drawers that were bursting with furs and scraps of luxurious fabric. Jumping, climbing, running, flipping, singing, and dancing, we would put on a show for my grandparents and tear apart their apartment.

Nonna relentlessly told me that it was beautiful to be young, and beautiful to be in love. She told me over and over to love life, a lesson that I am only now beginning to fully comprehend.

An Inheritance I'd Like to Return

A paradigm of scarcity and criticism. I was born into a world of scarcity. Before I could talk I had inherited rules about the world saying that there is not enough love and attention for everyone. I learned that I had to prove that I was worthy of love and so adopted a story that I was perpetually not good enough...or could always be better. The only way to be loved was to be the alpha, be the best.

This was amplified by an inheritance of criticism and perfection. I most clearly remember learning this from my maternal grandfather, my Nonno. He taught me to color in the lines, and to count by playing poker. His strict homework policies were quickly drilled into me. If anything was wrong with my homework, I had to start over. I know his intention was to help me succeed in life and be an intelligent woman who could become anything she wanted to be. One of the side effects, however, was that I learned to only be satisfied by perfection. I learned I would only be given positive attention and affection if I made no mistakes. Additionally, I learned that the judge who could approve my worthiness was an older male. Being flawless was rewarded, and everything else wasn't good enough.

While this rigor made me an honor roll student, it also made it very difficult for me to know who I was outside the approval of someone else. It is exhausting to chase my own tail of perfection, and to strive to meet the highest standards of everyone. Sadly, I learned to neglect judgment and my intuition. I ignored what I want, and who I am, because I distracted myself with mastery and accomplishment. Unlearning this, is one of my major life lessons.

What It Means to Be a Woman

My body is a doorway, a portal for human life. It blows my mind that the creative essence of the universe resides in my body. The potential for life is written into the fabric of my DNA. I can grow an entire universe inside of me. The future of our species literally is in my hands, my feet, my voice, and my womb. That is fucking amazing. Whether I have children or not, it is still damn incredible.

Being a woman means having more power than I can possibly comprehend. In the present time, it means discovering how to live authentically, believing in a paradigm of abundance, and relearning how to love myself. It means reclaiming my power and myself while the world around me tells me I shouldn't. It is soul retrieval in a hostile environment. But, I have faith I can, and will, and do.

Something I Regret

I deeply regret the cruelty and dominance I showed my younger sisters growing up. I would wield my physical, emotional, intellectual and social dominance over them. I wish I had known better, and I now see the effect it has had on them—suffering. I feel ashamed, and hope that one day they can forgive me. Until then, I strive to forgive myself. It wasn't female competition or sibling rivalry, it was bullying and oppression. I cannot expect to create a world that doesn't oppress women, until I can resolve the wounds I carry from being the oppressor.

What I Want to Get Out of Being a Woman

Self-liberation. Re-wilding. A declaration of inheritance and my own legacy. I want to be honored, celebrated, and appreciated for my authentic self and for the greatness that resides in every breath I take. I want to live and love fully, without apology. I want to show people a better way to be in relationship with one another. I want to treat myself as sacred and divine. I want to feel empowered by my physical, intellectual, social, emotional and cultural qualities. I want to teach the world to integrate the feminine. I want to have tea parties with joy and pleasure, and fire circles with adventure and wonder. I want to rage when it is time to rage, forgive when it is time to forgive, and grieve when it is time to grieve. I want to debunk the myth of scarcity. I want to have outrageously sexy and fulfilling relationships. I want to help other women know the importance and magnificence of their lives. I want to help women and men heal from the wounds of patriarchy.

The Legacy I Want to Live

My purpose is to lead the restoration of humanity. To illuminate multi-dimensional healing through cultivating and experiencing unconditional love and joy for self and others. I devote myself to lifelong learning, liberty, and the purposefulness, dignity and connectedness of all living beings. With a re-wilding femininity and a tenacious sense of adventure, I dance with the sacred and make miracles. My living legacy is to welcome, cultivate, and exemplify the potential of human relationships.

I want to be a living example of a better world. I hope I can inspire people to reconnect with their wholeness, purpose, and bliss. I hope people feel loved, unconditionally, when they are around me. I hope the *Inheritance* show becomes a landmark event and turning point in our collective consciousness. And, I hope this revolution thing works. For real.

YOUR STORY

I hope that these women's stories inspired you to explore and share your own. Each story of inheritance is unique and sacred. Each narrative offers the opportunity to see the similarities between us and to connect us in more authentic ways.

The first step to rewriting the legacy of women is to start with your story. Take the time to gently and intimately get to know your inheritance. When were your stories born? Under what circumstances were they forged? How do your stories work in your favor or inhibit you? What are the stories you wish you had now? What nutrients do your new narratives need to grow?

Storytelling is the playing field where vulnerability becomes strength. When you speak from this place, you transform from the inside-out. I invite you on this journey to not only examine and rewrite your story, but our collective narrative.

In the following pages, you will find weekly reflection questions to guide you. Move through them at your own pace with curiosity and compassion. Keep a journal to help record your reflections. The questions were designed to be reviewed sequentially, but let your intuition be your guide. Respond to what is speaking to you in the moment. Embrace your story. Own your story. Tell your story. Transform your story.

Week 1

Sit in a comfortable position. You may either sit in silence or listen to a soothing piece of music. With your eyes closed, begin focusing on your breath. For five minutes, be still. Notice any thoughts or emotions that become present.

I call this practice mindful self-awareness. I believe mindful self-awareness is a foundational building block to all communication, empowerment, leadership, and social change. Being able to identify and clearly communicate your experience is essential to changing it. Self-awareness includes your:

- Thoughts and judgments
- Feelings and emotions
- Somatic responses
- Intuitions
- Wants and needs
- Behaviors

Practice a self-awareness check-in now. In the present moment, what are you thinking, feeling, physical body sensations, intuitions, wants, needs, and actions? Write down your responses in your journal. You might be better at describing one aspect of your awareness over another. That is okay. Notice what your strengths are, and continue practicing the other areas of self-awareness.

Next, you will practice a free write. In a free write, you write for 10 minutes straight, without stopping. You may use the questions below as a guide, or write what comes up naturally for you in the moment. It is important that you keep writing, even if you must write "I can't think of anything else to write." Set a timer and begin.

Guiding Questions:
- What impact did reading these stories have on you?
- Which stories resonated with you the most? Why?

This week, look for opportunities to listen deeply to the stories of others. When you listen to their stories, see if you can distinguish their thoughts, feelings, wants, needs, and behaviors.

Week 2

Begin with a mindfulness meditation. Set a timer for five to ten minutes. Use this time to relax and become present. This week's activity will focus on describing who you are.

Next, write a self-awareness check-in in your journal. In the present moment, what are you thinking, feeling, physical body sensations, intuitions, wants, needs, and behaviors? After your check-in, use the guiding questions below for today's writing activity.

Guiding Questions:
- What are 20 words that describe you?
- What are you most proud of?
- What do you believe is your purpose in life?

This week, practice a self-awareness check-in every day.

Week 3

Begin with a five to ten minute mindfulness meditation and a self-awareness check-in.

Use the guiding questions below for today's writing activity.

Guiding Questions:
- Make a list of ten things you've inherited.
- What is something you've inherited that you like?
- What does it mean to you?
- What is your favorite piece of inheritance?
- What inheritance are you determined to pass on?

Close this reflection by writing another self-awareness check-in. This week, express your gratitude to the people who have given you an inheritance that you like.

Week 4

Begin with a five to ten minute mindfulness meditation and a self-awareness check-in.

Use the guiding questions below for today's writing activity.

Guiding Questions:
- What is something you've inherited that you don't like?
- What does it mean to you?
- How has it negatively influenced your life?

Close this reflection by writing another self-awareness check-in. This week continue to practice doing self-awareness check-ins every day.

Week 5

Begin with a five to ten minute mindfulness meditation and a self-awareness check-in.

Return to the list of 20 words you used to describe yourself. Take a moment to see if anything is missing from your list that you would like to add. Next, rank the words in order of how strongly you feel about them today. What are your top five? What are your top three? Use your top three and the guiding questions below for today's writing activity.

Guiding Questions:
- What does it mean to you to be _____, _____, and _____?
- What do you want to get out of being _____, _____, and _____?
- How do the top three words align to your purpose in life?

Close this reflection by writing a self-awareness check-in. This week, notice how the top three words that describe you are reinforced by others. For example, if you strongly identify with being a woman, how many times a day do you receive messages confirming that you are a woman?

Week 6

Begin with a five to ten minute mindfulness meditation and a self-awareness check-in.

Make a list of 20 words that you believe you are not. For example, you might think you are not weak, irresponsible, messy, etc. If you need help, refer to the previous list of 20 words that describe you—what is the opposite of those words? Once you have your list, take a moment to rank the words in order of how strongly you feel about them. What are the top five you feel most strongly about today; "I am *definitely* not..." What are the top three? Next, select the one you feel most strongly about today. Use this word and the guiding questions below for today's writing activity.

Guiding Questions:
- When is the first time you remember not wanting to be (insert your word here)?
- What would happen if you were (insert your word here)?
- When I think of being (insert your word here), I feel...
- When I think of being (insert your word here), these judgments come to mind...
- When I think of being (insert your word here), my body feels...
- When I think of being (insert your word here), I want to...
- What actions do I take every day to avoid being (insert your word here)?

Close this reflection by writing a self-awareness check-in, and give yourself five minutes of physical self-care. Stretch, walk, get a cool drink, etc. This week, practice a self-awareness check-in any time you are confronted with being called something you are not.

Week 7

Begin with a five to ten minute mindfulness meditation and a self-awareness check-in.

We are often bombarded with stories about who we should be or how we should behave. For this writing activity, make a list of as many 'shoulds' as you can, and who wanted you to inherit that 'should.' For example: 'I should be happy—my grandmother' or 'I should not ask for that raise—my coworker.' You can also include a list of the 'shoulds' that you think others should be, for example: 'My brother should be more financially responsible' or 'My roommate should be more careful.'

Once you have a list that feels complete, draw a picture of who you 'should' be and another picture of who you 'should not' be.

Close this reflection with a self-awareness check-in and 15 minutes of self-care. This week, notice how often you and others around you use the word 'should.'

Week 8

Begin with a five to ten minute mindfulness meditation and a self-awareness check-in.

Using the list of 'shoulds' you created previously, identify the top five you feel most strongly about. Next, select the top three. Finally, identify the one that you feel most strongly about today. Use the guided questions below for today's writing activity.

Guiding Questions:

- Where does that 'should' live in your body? Describe what it feels like.
- Who did you inherit this 'should' from?
- Why do you think (insert name of person) thinks you should/shouldn't be (insert quality here)?
- What are you risking by breaking the rules about who you 'should' be?
- What are three things you would start or stop doing if you no longer practiced this 'should?'

Close this reflection with a self-awareness check-in and 15 minutes of self-care. This week, practice a self-awareness check-in any time you use the word 'should.' During the check-in, pay special attention to identifying what you want and what you need.

Week 9

Begin with a five to ten minute mindfulness meditation and a self-awareness check-in.

In this activity you are going to examine a 'should' more closely. Select one you feel a strong emotional response to. When did this 'should' story begin? Use the guiding question below to craft an origin story for the 'should.'

Guided Questions:

- Describe the first time you learned this 'should' story.
- Describe the last time you remember this story being reinforced.
- Describe a time when you didn't abide by this 'should'—what happened?
- Explain how believing and reinforcing this 'should' story has served you.
- Explain how believing and reinforcing this 'should' story has inhibited you.
- What about this story do you want to change?

Close this reflection with a self-awareness check-in and 20 minutes of self-care. This week give yourself 20 minutes of self-care every day.

Week 10

Begin with a five to ten minute mindfulness meditation and a self-awareness check-in.

Regrets are a clue to identifying our legacy. By reflecting on your individual, familial, and cultural regrets, you can begin to clarify the legacy you want to live. Use the guiding questions below for today's writing activity.

Guiding Questions:
- What are five regrets you have?
- What regrets do you think your parents and grandparents have (your family of origin)?
- What regrets do you think your cultural of origin have? (national, religious, ethnic, etc.)
- Reviewing these regrets, what do you think, feel, need, and want?
- What would be different if you didn't hold these regrets?

Close by taking 20 minutes of self-care. If you experience regret this week, take time to journal about it and draw images that represent your experience.

Week 11

Begin with a five to ten minute mindfulness meditation and a self-awareness check-in. Then, use the guiding questions below for today's writing activity.

Guiding Questions:
- What legacy do you most want to pass on?
- What do you want people to think about you?
- How do you want people to feel about you?
- How do you want to feel about yourself?
- Why is this legacy important to you?
- If you succeed at living and leaving this legacy, what would the world look like around you? How would people be thinking, feeling, and behaving?
- Are there any differences in the legacy you want to leave versus the legacy you want to live? Explain.

This week, notice where and when you feel most aligned to your legacy. Note these times in your journal.

Week 12

Begin with a five to ten minute mindfulness meditation and a self-awareness check-in.

Today, you are going to create your own legacy dance. Make a list of the top four words you would use to describe the legacy you want to live. For each word you select, create a pose that represents it. Hold each pose for 30 seconds to really feel it in your body. Once you have four poses, practice moving from one pose to the next—you have created your very own legacy dance!

Close with a self-awareness check-in. Practice embodying your legacy throughout the week by repeating your legacy dance each day.

Week 13

Begin with a five to ten minute mindfulness meditation and a self-awareness check-in.

Taking the time to listen to yourself allows you to better hear others. Use the guiding questions below in today's writing activity.

Guiding Questions:
- What part of you needs to be listened to today?
- What does it want to say?
- What important information does it want you to know?
- What are the loud voices saying?
- What are the quiet voices saying?

Close this reflection with a check-in. Throughout the week, practice listening to yourself more closely.

Week 14

Begin with a five to ten minute mindfulness meditation and a self-awareness check-in.

Being seen for who you are, and seeing others for who they are is a healing action. Retrieve the list of words describing who you are, and who you are not. Write or draw them on the same paper as a beautiful landscape. When your landscape is complete, spend five interrupted minutes looking at yourself in the mirror. Use the guiding questions below in today's writing activity.

Guiding Questions:

- What do you notice looking at your landscape?
- How do you feel (physically and emotionally) after looking at your landscape?
- What wants or needs do you have after looking at your landscape?
- What actions do you want to take as a result of looking at your landscape?

Close with another mindfulness meditation. This week, practice self-awareness check-ins at least twice a day.

Week 15

Begin with a five to ten minute mindfulness meditation and a self-awareness check-in.

Committing to a change is the next step. I challenge you to make a daring and tenacious commitment. I challenge you to stop doing something, permanently...now. Don't plan to stop next week, or after the new year. Demand it from yourself from this moment forward. Be bold. Take a moment to review your journal entries. Identify and let go of a story you've inherited that no longer serves you. Thank it for serving you all these years, and then release it with dignity.

Guiding Questions:
- The story I am letting go of is ...
- This story has helped me in the past by...
- I am letting go of this story now because...
- Releasing this story helps me live more aligned to my legacy by...
- When I think of letting go of this story, I feel...

Over the course of the week, notice if this story tries to reunite with you. Gently remind it that you have let it go. Share your commitment with at least three people.

Week 16

Begin with a five to ten minute mindfulness meditation and a self-awareness check-in.

Today, you will make a bold commitment to start something that promotes your value, worth, self-acceptance, and self-love. You will begin this commitment immediately, and it will help you align more with the legacy you want to live.

Guiding Questions:
- Today I will start....
- Beginning _____ will help me align to my legacy by....
- Beginning _____ will help change the world by...
- If I need help continuing this commitment along the way, I will ...

This week, notice how many opportunities there are for you to practice what you committed to starting. Share your commitment with at least three people.

ABOUT THE AUTHOR

Cat Cuevas, MA in an international trainer, consultant, speaker and performer. She has been a teacher, NCAA coach, camp director, adjunct professor, business owner, CEO and CLO of a start-up benefit corporation, and show producer. Her greatest challenge and accomplishment has been the process of self-liberation and self-love. Cat specializes in helping people develop the cognitive, emotional, social, spiritual, intuitive, organizational, and cultural behaviors needed to facilitate systemic transformational change. Cat has a MA in International Peace and Conflict Resolution, and a MA in Leadership and Organizational Development. She has, however, learned more about business and leadership from being an exotic dancer than all the books and journals she's read. Cat loves choreographing poignant, playful, and dynamic learning for her clients that restores joy, wellness, and wholeness. She is on a mission to exalt feminine leadership. Learn more at www.catcuevas.com.